THINGS THAT GO

BOATS EDITION

BABY PROFESSOR

EDUCATION KIDS

Long before there were cars or even wagons and carts, people used boats to get around and travel.

A boat is a watercraft of any size designed to float on water, whether it be in lakes, rivers or seas.

Boats have a wide variety of shapes and sizes and construction methods due to their intended purpose, available materials or local traditions.

Dugouts are
the oldest type
of boats that
archaeologists
have found.

Simple dugouts have been known since prehistoric times to all peoples dwelling on waterways.

Boats can be categorized into three main types; Unpowered or human-powered boats, Sailboats and Motorboats.

Unpowered boats include rafts and floats meant for one-way downstream travel. Human-powered boats include kayaks, canoes and gondolas and boats propelled by poles.

Sailboats are propelled by wind and sails. The tall upright post on a sailboat is called a mast.

Motorboats are propelled by mechanical means, such as engines. Some motorboats are fitted with inboard engines, others have an outboard motor installed on the rear.

Nearly every boat is given a name by the owner, and this is how the boat is referred to in the boating community, and in some cases, in legal or title paperwork.

The boat's left side is referred to as the port side. The boat's right side is referred to as the starboard side. The bow is the boats front, and the boat's back is called the stern.

There are approximately 18 million boats owned by Americans for recreational use today. Boating is ranked in the top 3 for stress relieving activities.

A lifeboat is a
boat designed
to save lives
of people in
trouble at sea.

A tugboat is
a boat that
maneuvers
vessels by
pushing or towing
them. Some
tugboats serve
as icebreakers or
salvage boats.